Can You Change If You're Gay?

David White

....

New
Growth
Press
www.newgrowthpress.com

New Growth Press, Greensboro, NC 27404
www.newgrowthpress.com
Copyright © 2013 by Harvest USA

All Scripture quotations, unless otherwise indicated are from *The Holy Bible, English Standard Version*® (ESV®), copyright © 2000, 2001 by Crossway Bibles, a division of Good News Publishers. Used by permission. All rights reserved.

Scripture quotations marked NIV are taken from the *Holy Bible, New International Version*®, NIV®. Copyright © 1973, 1978, 1984, 2011 by Biblica, Inc. Used by permission. All rights reserved worldwide.

Cover Design: Faceout books, faceout.com
Typesetting: Lisa Parnell, lparnell.com

ISBN-10: 1-939946-07-7
ISBN-13: 978-1-939946-07-2

Library of Congress Cataloging-in-Publication Data
White, David, 1970–
   Can you change if you're gay? / author David White.
      pages cm.
   Includes bibliographical references and index.
   ISBN 978-1-939946-07-2 (alk. paper)
   1. Homosexuality—Religious aspects—Christianity. I. Title.
BR115.H6W445 2013
261.8'35766—dc23   2013023728

Printed in Canada

21 20 19 18 17 16 15 14   2 3 4 5 6

*Dedicated to my brothers and sisters living
in self-denial because they believe the promises
and know He is better. The world is not worthy
of you. Your sacrificial obedience is an inheritance that
is imperishable, undefiled, and unfading. Press on!*

"I love children. I've always wanted a family. I just can't imagine myself ever getting married. I mean, how would sex even *work*?!" Exhaling through pursed lips, Frank wipes the corner of his eye. "I don't think this is working."

A Christian in his early thirties, wrestling with same-sex attraction (SSA), he has been beaten down by the relentlessness of his temptation and his seeming inability to *change*. Like most people struggling with SSA, Frank hoped counseling and participation in a biblical support group would translate into deliverance from homosexual desires. For him, defeating SSA meant eradicating ongoing homosexual temptation and becoming heterosexual. This defines "change" for many people, and anything falling short feels like a "bait and switch."

"Women are tender and compassionate. They want to know me and actually care about the details of my life." With a bitter smile, Sue explains that she has never been physically attracted to men. Even worse, her experience as a survivor of sexual abuse means men feel radically unsafe. Relationships with women are so different. Compared to her horrific experience of male lust, intimacy with a woman feels nurturing and safe. "I have no desire to marry. A relationship with a man has zero appeal for me. Why can't I experience love the way I want?"

Unlike Frank, Sue doesn't really care about changing her sexual orientation. These days she has lots of support. Many (most?) people today believe that sexual orientation is inborn and unchangeable. They want freedom to follow their desires without expectation to conform to traditional understandings of love, relationships, and community.

Others believe that changing your sexual orientation is as simple as changing your circumstances. "I thought marriage would make a difference. I assumed a 'God-approved' outlet for sexual release would just, you know, change the wiring." Shaking his head and throwing up his hands in exasperation, George lamented, "The temptations have never gone away. Physical intimacy is challenging. I never knew this would be so *hard*." Some people place false hope in solutions that seem to promise change. Often they are spurred on by well-meaning people who don't understand the depth of these issues and a biblical definition of change.

The ongoing, persistent nature of SSA is extremely difficult for those who want to uphold God's design for sexuality. There is a reason so many prominent Christians "come out" or depart from biblical standards when a loved one discloses their struggle. For the vast majority, SSA will be a lifelong experience in this fallen world. It is a unique and, at times, excruciating burden to bear, but it is not a hopeless journey. If this is your struggle, be assured that God wants to meet you. He often brings us to desolate, wilderness places to "allure" us, speak tenderly to us, reveal the depth of his love, and draw us closer as his beloved people (see Hosea 1–3, especially 2:14–23).

Conflicting Views of Change

There are many cultural voices expressing wildly divergent perspectives on change. Because the media shouts the loudest, a growing number of people believe SSA is "inborn and unchangeable." After all, no one ever asked to be this way. The desires are not by conscious choice. They come unbidden and stubbornly persist. Although direct genetic and/or physiological origins remain scientifically unproven, the culture insists that altering sexual orientation is as futile as trying to change skin color. The very attempt is labeled psychologically harmful, so California recently made it illegal for therapists to talk to teenagers about the possibility of change.[1] In the wake of the media onslaught and mounting social pressure, many claiming to follow Jesus have abandoned the Bible's clear teaching on human sexuality.

Sadly, even the church's voice is frequently unhelpful. First, homosexuality is often viewed as particularly abhorrent and far worse than heterosexual brokenness. Many with SSA grew up in the church hearing only messages of condemnation, living in dread of judgment because of the nature of their temptations. Further, some Christians don't understand the complexity of SSA. They act like it is simply a chosen "lifestyle" that can be easily deselected. Perhaps more pervasive is a triumphalist Christianity suggesting any significant sin struggle is overcome as long as someone has enough faith. Consider the typical church testimony: "My life was a mess. Then I got saved. Now everything's great!" Anything short of painless, temptation-free, easy obedience is chalked up to an individual's failure to *really* believe, as if this life is a pleasant Sunday stroll heavenward.

Finally, most people (particularly those struggling) see change as nothing less than the utter eradication of

SSA, coupled with a big boost in heterosexual desire. Mistakenly, they look to traditional marriage, children, a house in the 'burbs with a white picket fence, and grandchildren in due time. There is an understandable longing for relief from unwanted attractions and ongoing temptation, but this expectation goes far beyond the promises of the Bible. How can we sort through all the dissonant voices?

Who Needs Change?

Not surprisingly, the Bible's perspective on change differs from all the voices above. First, the inborn and unchangeable claim rests on cultural worldview and personal experience, not science, and certainly not on biblical revelation.[2] The argument goes, "I never asked for SSA. I've always felt this way. It is natural for me. Therefore, God made me this way." The entire superstructure of pro-gay theology rests on this "sandy" foundation.

Here's the rub: the Bible teaches that what is "natural" to us is broken. The fall of humanity into sin led to a fundamental disordering of the world. All of creation is "groaning" under the curse, longing for redemption (Romans 8:20–22). Nothing in this world is the way it's supposed to be. All of us have a broken sexuality in need of redemption. No one goes through life with blinders on and a dormant sexuality until they finally meet that special someone of the opposite sex, get married, and spend the rest of their lives in starry-eyed, selfless devotion, never looking to the left or right. In a fallen world, sexuality is bent in innumerable directions. All of us have a broken sexuality. My wedding ring is completely foreign to me naturally. Apart from Christ, I was unfaithful in every "exclusive" relationship. I'm not naturally wired for monogamy—I needed a radical, *supernatural* intervention to overcome my "natural" tendencies.

Beginning in Genesis 3 and running straight through to Revelation, the Bible assumes our "natural" state is broken and anti-God, meaning we live for self, not him (see Romans 3:9–20 for the most succinct description of our desperate plight). This is humanity's natural "orientation"—to live self-determinative, autonomous lives apart from God. Who we are naturally is *not* God-given! Our feelings, our attractions, and the worldviews we develop as we are shaped by life can't be trusted. Thus the very starting point of pro-gay theology is completely unbiblical. As C. S. Lewis wrote, "Fallen man is not simply an imperfect creature who needs improvement: he is a rebel who must lay down his arms."[3]

In our pluralist society, many choose to reject the Bible's perspective on humanity, but for any who call their faith *Christian*, our broken natural state, our utter inability to change ourselves and our desperate need for God's supernatural intervention is the only starting point for understanding what is wrong with us (and the world at large!). Embracing the hard truth about humanity is where change begins. All of humanity needs a changed sexuality!

A New Focus for Change

Since Freud, our culture has overemphasized the importance of sexuality. Many women wrestle intensely with body image because they are inundated by the lie that sex appeal is one of the most important aspects of their person. In this environment, it's not surprising that people build their fundamental identity around sexuality. While not denying that sexuality is important, consider how building your *identity* around it tragically diminishes what it means to be human. The Bible gives two primary categories for identity-formation, which are tied to the reality that we are body and spirit. Physically, we are created male or female in God's "image," and spiritually, we are either "in Christ" or not.

Both the physical and spiritual aspects of our person are focused on our relationship to God. The intent is for our identity to be completely bound up in him— our Creator and Redeemer. This relational identity is of infinitely greater worth than sexual orientation. It is the core identity for a Christian. That's why it's troubling that a growing number of Christians uphold biblical sexual morality in practice, but adopt the identity of "celibate, gay Christian." Our struggles *do* matter because they initially shape our understanding of ourselves, God, and our relationships with others. But in this ongoing journey in which we develop and grow, we need to be wary of these adjectives lest we become stuck and don't mature beyond our own self-description.

God invites us to be defined in Christ and the beauty of our ongoing, growing redemption in him. Better to acknowledge our struggle, but not embrace SSA as an identity. The concern here is that brothers and sisters in Christ may define themselves too narrowly. It is helpful for others to hear of our struggles and commitment to submit to Christ—comforting others with the comfort we've received (2 Corinthians 1:3–4)—but let's be careful how we describe ourselves. The narrow definition puts us on the "wrong turf"—using the world's descriptions of humanity instead of celebrating God's redemption. I'd have a similar concern if someone with a history of substance abuse described himself as a "dry, alcoholic Christian." Let's be defined by the wonder of who we are as the people of God!

Christians considering "change" and SSA must think in biblical categories. According to the Bible, the allegiance of our hearts is the biggest area needing change. The essence of the gospel is that although we were his enemies, God reconciled us to himself through Christ, not counting our sins against us (2 Corinthians 5:14–21). God initiated relationship with us and that becomes our core identity. "Who I am" is no longer based on my sexual attractions, desires, or behaviors. Increasingly, it's not on *me* at all—my life is radically reoriented around him. Ironically, God's created intent of romantic love is to point to this greater reality, this ultimate relationship (Ephesians 5:31–32). The way lovers (at least while "falling in love") abandon their self-interest for the sake of their beloved, beautifully reflects (as in a mirror dimly) God's self-giving love toward us in Christ and invites us to respond similarly.

Second Corinthians 5:14–15 powerfully describes this reality: "For the love of Christ controls us, because we have concluded this: that one has died for all, therefore all have died; and he died for all, that those who live might *no longer live for themselves but for him* who for their sake died and was raised" (emphasis added). The beloved of God in Christ becomes our identity and the controlling factor in our lives. In Jesus, we find the "treasure in the field," the "pearl of great value," and everything formerly prized is counted "as loss because of the surpassing worth of knowing Christ Jesus my Lord" (Matthew 13:44–46; Philippians 3:8).

The opposite of homosexuality isn't heterosexuality—it is *holiness*. To be holy means to be set apart for God. This is what it means that we are reconciled to him. He is our God, and we are his people. To be a disciple means taking up a cross, willing to lose my life for his sake, believing his promise that in so doing I will actually find abundant life. Thus Dietrich Bonhoeffer wrote, "When Christ calls a man, he bids him come and die."[4]

A Biblical View of Change

The hope of the gospel is that God does what is impossible for us: he gives us a new heart that understands our need for his grace and embraces Christ by faith. The Holy Spirit at work in this new heart enables us to obey. And, as we examined above, obedience flows from *affection* for God in response to his love for us. Although the new heart we are given when we come to Christ by faith is "instantaneous," the outworking in our lives is a lifelong process.

The truth is that temptation, struggle, and loss will be a lifelong reality, not just for the SSA struggler, but for everyone who lives in this fallen world. Jesus taught in this world we would have trouble, but we can take heart because he has overcome the world (John 16:33). Although it is necessary that temptation comes (Matthew 18:7), God promises that all the trials and suffering in this life have purpose (James 1:2–4; 1 Peter 1:6–8). He promises there will always be a way out of temptation so we are able to *endure* it (1 Corinthians 10:13).

So to speak of change biblically means in Christ we now have the ability to obey God, aligning our life to his will and design. Transformation means I am no longer a slave to my desires. By his Spirit, God empowers us to obey—in the face of ongoing temptation and the tug of our flesh. Listen to how Paul describes this battle: "For the desires of the flesh are against the Spirit, and the desires of the Spirit are against the flesh, for these are opposed to each other, to keep you from doing the things you want to do" (Galatians 5:17). As we live in relationship with him, and equally important, as we live authentically with others in the community of Christ, the Spirit of God reins us in and, even though we "want" to continue pursuing sinful activities, his hand restrains us in love as we surrender to him. In fact, the relational aspect of our faith is so important that living in obedience is described as the demonstration that we know Christ (1 John 2:1–5). In other words, when we know him and experience the blessing of that relationship, we obey. Not because it's easy, but because he is worth it.

Change in daily life

If biblical change is not about sexual orientation, how does it work out practically in your daily life? There are five important categories to consider: sexuality, community, same-sex friendships, our definition of "victory," and our hope for enduring, life-long temptation.

Changed perspective of sexuality

God wants to change our perspective on sex. He wants us to learn that all of life, including our sexuality, is ultimately about knowing, following, and glorifying him. First Thessalonians 4:1–8 poignantly links our sexuality with our spirituality, teaching that sexual behavior reveals the allegiance of our hearts. Christians are supposed to exercise self-control in this area because out of control/out of bounds sexuality is what unbelievers do. Why does God want our sexuality to be exclusive, expressed only within the bounds of his design? Briefly, God created marriage and sexuality to give us a glimpse of himself and his relationship with us. Thus Paul, in describing marriage says, "This mystery is profound, and I am saying that it refers to Christ and the church" (Ephesians 5:32). God calls us to radical sexual fidelity within marriage because it is intended to mirror our radical spiritual fidelity to him (and his fidelity to us, his "bride"). Scripture describes idolatry as adultery because this is the closest human experience that approximates God's heartache over sin.

The issue is not whether we are heterosexual or homosexual or any other prefix of your choice. Remember, the opposite of homosexuality is not heterosexuality, but *holiness*. Ultimately, we are called to be Christo-sexual. We submit our desires and affections to Jesus, learning how to manage our bodies "in holiness." Sex in marriage—at its glorious, God-ordained best—is more than physical: it points beyond itself, anticipating the great consummation of the Wedding Feast of the Lamb (Revelation 19:6–10). Further, sex in marriage is a gift that catches just a glimpse of the reality that living forever in the presence of God is "fullness of joy; at your right hand are pleasures forevermore" (Psalm 16:11). God is not about squashing our pleasures. He wants us to experience true pleasures, which are centered in relationship to him.

For singles, this means joining Jesus in *fasting*, believing he is our ultimate Bridegroom (more on this below). He understands the grace you need to be faithful because he faced every temptation you face *victoriously* (Hebrews 4:15). Can you see your unsatisfied sexual longings as a reflection of his longing for you? It is possible for even our lust to turn to worship as we embrace him, rather than satisfying our flesh. He is delighted by this sacrificial obedience. He promises "no good thing does he withhold from those who walk uprightly" (Psalm 84:11). Anything sacrificed for the sake of Christ will be restored to you a hundredfold. On the Last Day, no one will look back and wish they had more sex. God has pleasures in store for us that he says we can't even begin to imagine. I suspect we need a resurrection body to even take them in—our current bodies couldn't handle it!

Similarly, married people are called to be "Christo-spousal-sexual," meaning husbands and wives are to submit their sexuality to Christ and be committed to serving the desires of their spouse. Even those who are married need to learn to manage their bodies "in holiness"! Further, God calls married people to be "spousal-sexual," having a single individual (yes, of the opposite sex) be the recipient of all sexual longing and expression. And the goal of physical intimacy is to selflessly serve and bring pleasure to the other (1 Corinthians 7:1–5). This is radically countercultural and against nature for all of us in a fallen world.

So, it isn't sufficient for people with SSA to begin experiencing heterosexual desire, get married, and perform heterosexually. (And perhaps begin struggling with heterosexual lust!) Making heterosexuality the goal for SSA falls so far short of God's plan. There needs to be a *greater* redemption of our sexuality. Christ-centered sexuality is about submitting our sexual desires, longings, and affections to him, and learning by his power to live "in holiness" within his good and perfect design. Is this easy? No. Is it possible? Yes. By his grace that transforms every human heart that comes to him, and by the means that are further expressed below, SSA Christians can change to faithfully follow Christ.

Changed approach to community

One man described himself saying, "I used to be tin foil, now I'm plastic wrap." What does he mean? Formerly, he lived a life of hiding. For decades no one knew about his struggle with sexual sin. It was safely hidden behind the façade of Christian husband, father, and successful businessman. His deepest struggle and pain was neatly wrapped beneath an opaque covering—careful to keep the shiny side outward. Although he made some strides—

turning away from porn and solo sex—he lived in bondage to uncontrolled thoughts and the crippling fear of exposure, not to mention the inner anguish that comes from not being truly *known* by others—including his wife.

In stark contrast, he is now "plastic wrap." He is known by others. A particularly encouraging ministry experience was speaking at a men's breakfast at his church where he shared his testimony. I had spoken at his church years earlier, and he was shocked that anyone could stand in front of a group of men candidly discussing sexual sin and the difference Jesus makes in the battle. It had come full circle— *he* was up front, before the brothers from his own church, sharing about where he'd been and what God was doing in his life. This is radical transformation!

It is heartbreaking to hear of Christians "coming out" after living with a secret struggle for years. In our guilt and shame we are desperate to stay hidden. Either isolation or plastic smiles tend to characterize men and women struggling with SSA or sexual sin in the church. Both are crushing to the soul because we are created to be in relationship and experience intimacy with others. Remember that it was not good for Adam to be alone. This doesn't mean every person needs to marry, but it does mean every person needs community! The gospel invites you to come out of hiding because God promises if you trust in him you will *never* be put to shame. You will not be left naked; he will clothe you with the righteousness of Christ. 1 John 1:5–10 promises "if we walk in the light" (choosing a life of openness instead of hiding), we will have fellowship with others and find increasing freedom from our struggles with sin. Where do we begin?

1) Pray. Ask God to open your eyes to the people around you who are "safe," with whom you can

open your heart. Ask him for wisdom about timing and for opportunities to share. Pray for courage. I can't tell you how many people come back rejoicing because they faced their fears and began to open this issue to others.

2) Talk to your pastor. Your pastor should be the safest person for you to share your sin struggles with. If this is *not* the case, you need to ask yourself whether you are in the right church. If you regularly hear messages that condemn homosexuality as somehow worse than other sins, or "It's Adam & Eve, not Adam & Steve" banter, then it may not be a safe place. But in most cases, I would encourage you to risk talking with your pastor. Give him the benefit of the doubt before you start "church shopping."

3) Or approach a lay spiritual leader. Assuming the same disclaimers given above, many churches have home Bible studies with these leaders often functioning as the direct shepherds of God's people. Especially if you are in a large church, this may be the most appropriate spiritual leader to talk with.

4) Let existing friends into your places of struggle. Admittedly, this significantly "ups the ante." Pastors and other ministry leaders *have* to accept us, but friends can reject us. Yet, it is in these relationships where we most long to be known, and maintaining a façade is all the more painful. You will always doubt the sincerity of the friendship and shame will always dog you until you risk exposing the worst things about yourself.

5) Share with your family. It is crucial to underscore again the importance of prayer! Many experience deeply broken family relationships that are the

antithesis of "safe." However, others stay silent out of fear or pride. The result is a deepening sense of estrangement or rejection, especially if SSA is disparagingly discussed at family gatherings. Parents and siblings are often deeply distraught over careless comments made prior to knowing their loved one's struggle. Although initially terrifying, many testify that disclosing their struggle with SSA to their family was used by God to free them from decades of fear and shame.

God designed his people to live inter-dependently. The New Testament describes us as body parts "nourished and knit together," connected to our Head, Jesus Christ, growing "with a growth that is from God" (Colossians 2:19). We only reach maturity as "each part is working properly" (Ephesians 4:16). People can only encourage you if they know the places you are *discouraged*. Lives begin to change when others are invited into our struggles. And for people who lived in posturing or isolation, this is radical life change indeed!

Changed experience of same-sex friendships

"I am distressed for you, my brother Jonathan; very pleasant have you been to me; your love to me was extraordinary, surpassing the love of women" (2 Samuel 1:26). This is King David's lament over the death in battle of his best friend, Jonathan. With all same-sex friendships in the Bible (including Jesus and John), pro-gay theologians hunt for evidence of same-sex eroticism. For them, David's comparison to "the love of women" is proof that David and Jonathan were sexually involved. This argument demonstrates the importance of this next area of change.

As mentioned above, sexuality in our culture is a defining factor of personal identity. The assumption follows that sexual experience is the pinnacle of human existence. That means denying sexual desires or choosing celibacy results in a shrunken existence. Denied a romantic, same-sex relationship, one man concluded, "If what you say is true, then my life can only be lonely and sad." What is his underlying assumption? Real joy and true companionship is *only* found in a sexual relationship. Our distorted, sex-obsessed culture can't begin to conceive of a nonsexual, same-sex friendship like that of David and Jonathan, where the bond of brotherhood (or sisterhood) is deeper than sex.

To the great detriment of our society, we've lost the wonder and power of *friendship*. In *The Four Loves*, Lewis contrasts sexual love that is inwardly focused on the couple's relationship, with friendship, described as two people standing side-by-side, looking beyond themselves at something else. Their unity is based on something outside the relationship. SSA strugglers in the body of Christ have the opportunity to experience the blessing of joy and satisfaction in non-sexual friendships. And this is not some relational "consolation prize." A stirring passage in *All Quiet on the Western Front* describes the intimacy among soldiers as closer than lovers. The threat of constant death birthed relationships transcending sex.

From the very beginning God declared it was "not good" for humanity to live alone, yet the answer is not that everyone should marry. Jesus said some would be "eunuchs" for the sake of the kingdom (Matthew 19:11–12). Paul urged Christians to refrain from marriage for the same reason (1 Corinthians 7:29–35). Either God is a killjoy, or sex is *not* the ultimate experience of life! The reason Jesus and Paul steered away from making marriage normative for all is that the ultimate Bridegroom has come and a new community (his bride) has been formed. Despite her flaws, the church is united by our love for him, the desire to proclaim and extend his kingdom, and the anticipation of our ultimate home. There is no Jew or Greek, slave or free, male or female because we are united in Christ (Galatians 3:28).

It is hard to live with unsatisfied desires, but sex is not life-giving in and of itself. The church needs to be at the forefront of rediscovering the blessing of community and friendship. God always promised to place "the lonely in families" (Psalm 68:6 NIV) and this should find its greatest fruition within the body of Christ. The choice isn't between a romantic relationship or loneliness. As Christians, we are invited into rich fellowship. People struggling with SSA are longing for emotional connection with others and often their thwarted desires are sexualized. Individuals find significant healing as they persevere in developing healthy relationships with others. Nevertheless, there are some unique challenges requiring wisdom for SSA strugglers pursuing same-sex friendships.

1) It probably doesn't make sense to pursue a close, intimate relationship with someone you find especially attractive. This is particularly true for men who may be more visually wired. However, many men say attraction dissipates over time. As they get to know someone—warts and all—the idealized, sexualized man on the pedestal is brought down to reality.

2) Avoid looking for a "best friend." Potentially a deep longing for people with SSA, but this intensity of relationship often excludes others, inviting

overdependence on an individual. Even as one flesh in marriage, a couple should never be an "island." All relationships should exist in the context of broader community. A "best friend" relationship, even if never sexualized, often prevents you from developing a larger base of relationships.

3) Instead, cultivate a network of multilayered relationships. It's healthy to have close friends, good friends, warm acquaintances, and others known only by name. It seems that in his earthly life even Jesus had varying levels of relationship: crowds who followed him, seventy-two sent out, twelve disciples who were with him from the beginning, three invited to witness the transfiguration and his agony in Gethsemane, and John, "the disciple Jesus loved," who reclined against him at the Last Supper.

I am blessed with Christian brothers I describe as "vital relationships." They keep me sane, help me see blind spots, spur me on in loving my family, and most importantly, point me to Christ when I am drowning in guilt and shame or pride and self-righteousness. *I would not still be in ministry today if I did not have these men in my life!* And whenever we meet in a coffee shop to talk and pray, we greet with a hug, despite the raised eyebrows, because people need to know that same-sex friendship is still alive and well.

Changed definition of victory

My colleague went to Disney World, returning with a magic wand. Why? That's what so many people with SSA desire. During college I worked as a waiter in Philadelphia.

I had many gay coworkers, and you know what they'd tell me? "If there was a pill that would make me straight, I'd take it!" Out and proud, living the gay life to the hilt, they were not laboring under religious guilt—but it wasn't working. As an unbeliever at the time, that stuck with me. Despite the pro-gay messages I was fed by culture, the real people I met with SSA longed to be free.

Here's the problem: we all want the "pill." We want Christianity without the challenge of obedience, without the tug of our flesh. We wish that life in this world was easier. We want the triumphalist version of the Christian life to be our experience. But Scripture never promises this. To the contrary, Jesus warned that discipleship means carrying a cross.

Just as change is understood as the eradication of temptation, so victory is often seen as a perfect track record. Although transformation is at the heart of the gospel, it is a process that takes time and is often marked by failure. In *Mere Christianity*, Lewis describes how we continually fall at the outset of our battle with lust. It's as if we haven't received enough grace. But failures are important because we learn to repent. Repeatedly returning to God for mercy, then rousing ourselves to start the fight of faith again, is important spiritual training. A crucial aspect of change is facing the worst in ourselves and doggedly clinging to Christ as our only hope.

This is victory! Confronting our failures honestly without excuses, justification, blameshifting, etc., reflects significant change. And the paradox of Christianity is that the deeper we understand our sin the sweeter the gospel grows, and then change happens. Victory ensues from acknowledging failure and increasingly resisting temptation because you grow in *knowing him*. You rest in who he is and what he has done for you and increasingly trust what he says about you. The Bible teaches that ultimate life change and victory only come through his grace (Titus 2:11–14). This is the fount of true, lifelong victory.

Changed Hope for Endurance

Further, God offers a different hope. SSA strugglers often focus on a transformed "orientation" because it is incredibly hard to imagine life without sex. For ten years I taught that sexuality's glory and ecstasy is ultimately about Jesus. When my wife passed away suddenly, he called me to *live it*. For three years I was celibate, bringing my longing to him. It was painful, but I discovered that he is enough. He satisfied my soul. Despite grief, loneliness, and times of intense longing, I experienced a fullness and richness in life.

Despite earthly blessings, our ultimate hope is not in this world. Growing in grace, our longing is increasingly for him. Heaven is not merely escaping the pain of this world, it's—at long last!—seeing him face-to-face. Hebrews 12:1 was a great encouragement in my grief. Building off the Hebrews 11 recounting of Old Testament saints, it declares we are surrounded by a "great cloud of witnesses." What might they say to us? "Hang in there. It's not as long as it seems in your daily battle with temptation. In a mere breath you'll be with us. And he's *worth it*."

Abraham doesn't wish he stayed in his father's house instead of living in tents. Moses doesn't regret forsaking the pleasures of sin in Egypt. Describing the desolation, persecution, and even horrific martyrdom of these ancient saints the passage declares "the world was not worthy of them" (Hebrews 11:36–38). Having entered his presence, they know the fullness of joy. They're experiencing the eternal pleasures found only at his right hand. They turned from the pleasures of this world and they have no regrets!

Perhaps you, too, are suffering ridicule. People can't understand why you deny yourself. You're labeled a fool and warned life is slipping through your fingers. It's true; this life is fleeting. But not only are you counted among those of whom this world is not worthy, there is a promised world coming that is literally beyond your ability to imagine. On the Last Day no one will look back and regret sacrificing their desires for his sake. The idea of missing out on sex will be ridiculous. There are pleasures and delights beyond our comprehension that are *eternal*. Even the earthly pleasures given by God are fleeting, pointing beyond themselves. He wants you to know pleasures that are eternal and pure. And they will all begin when he personally comes to you and wipes away every tear from your eye. Persevere because he is worth it!

Looking to the One Who Empowers Change

Finally, you need to know Jesus understands. Living with lifelong temptation can at times feel crushing, but *it gets better*. It will not always be as hard as it may be currently. Think about this: if there's a predator after you, it makes a huge difference whether it's a lion or a gnat. One destroys your life; the other is just a nuisance. As you walk in obedience, temptation becomes less life-dominating, more an annoyance than a destructive threat. As you turn from sinful behaviors that perpetuate SSA (porn, hookups, enmeshed relationships, etc.), reality grows clearer. The hook under temptation's bait becomes easier to spot, and you learn to identify and avoid it. More importantly, you experience "abundant life" in your relationship with God and others—relationships that can be deep, enriching, and need not be sexualized.

In following Christ, some people experience a lessening of SSA attractions over time, others do not. Some experience growth in heterosexual desires (especially toward a specific person they love), but some never experience this change. You won't necessarily develop romantic affections toward the opposite sex, but you will grow in your affection for Christ, your ultimate Bridegroom. Ultimately, "change" is the Spirit-led ability to resist and turn from temptation, and anyone in Christ can grow along that trajectory.

As I mentioned above, after the loss of my first wife, God met me in my grief, loneliness, and longing as never before. At one point, reading through Matthew, two passages jumped out. First, speaking of his return, Jesus declared that he did not know the day or hour—only the Father knows. Consider that. For two thousand years Jesus has waited, perhaps wondering with each new morning, "Is it today?" He has been waiting a *long* time. This is not to diminish your time of waiting. Rather, know that he knows what it takes for you to wait. He knows exactly the grace you need as you are daily waiting on him, trusting as he works change and growth in your life according to his timing. He is still waiting with you.

Secondly, at the Last Supper, Jesus passed the cup saying it would be the last time he would drink of the fruit of the vine until he drank it with us in the kingdom. He left us the Supper, telling us to partake frequently, remembering him until he returns—while he himself *fasts* from this cup of celebration. Even as Scripture depicts him as our victorious King, ruling the universe by the word of his power, Jesus still lives in self-denial. He is a waiting and fasting king. He is patient, but eagerly looking forward to sitting down at the wedding feast with you and me, at the marriage arranged by our Father from the foundation of the world.

Endnotes

1. http://www.nytimes.com/2012/10/01/us/california-bans-therapies-to-cure-gay-minors.html?_r=0 Accessed on March 24, 2013. Although I am not an advocate of "reparative therapy," the current legislative trend is concerning.

2. Even if science found genetic (or any other) predispositions to SSA, as they have with alcoholism and anger, the Bible is our ultimate authority for determining moral behavior.

3. C. S. Lewis, *Mere Christianity* (New York: Harper Collins, 1952/2001), 56.

4. Dietrich Bonhoeffer, *The Cost of Discipleship* (New York: Touchstone, 1959/1995), 89.